GAME-CHANGING QUARTERBACKS

CALEB WILLIAMS

Gareth Stevens PUBLISHING

BY P. J. FREEDMAN

HOT TOPICS

Please visit our website, www.garethstevens.com. For a free color catalog of all our high-quality books, call toll free 1-800-542-2595 or fax 1-877-542-2596.

Library of Congress Cataloging-in-Publication Data
Names: Freedman, P. J., author.
Title: Caleb Williams / P.J. Freedman.
Description: Buffalo, New York : Gareth Stevens Publishing, 2026. | Series: Game-changing quarterbacks | Includes index.
Identifiers: LCCN 2024052335 (print) | LCCN 2024052336 (ebook) | ISBN 9781482472417 (library binding) | ISBN 9781482472400 (paperback) | ISBN 9781482472424 (ebook)
Subjects: LCSH: Williams, Caleb, 2001—Juvenile literature. | Quarterbacks (Football)–United States–Biography–Juvenile literature. | Football players–United States–Biography–Juvenile literature.
Classification: LCC GV939.W487 F74 2026 (print) | LCC GV939.W487 (ebook) | DDC 796.332092 [B]–dc23/eng/20241211
LC record available at https://lccn.loc.gov/2024052335
LC ebook record available at https://lccn.loc.gov/2024052336

Published in 2026 by
Gareth Stevens Publishing
2544 Clinton Street
Buffalo, NY 14224

Cover Designer: Nicholas Switalski
Interior Designer: Rachel Rising
Editor: Kristen Nelson

Photo credits: Cover, p. 5 Cal Sport Media / Alamy Stock Photo; Back Cover EFKS/Shutterstock.com; pp. 3-32 swissdrone/Shutterstock.com; pp. 3, 4, 6, 8, 10, 12, 14, 16, 18, 20, 22, 24, 26, 28, 30, 32 Logvin art/Shutterstock.com; pp. 4, 7, 8, 10, 13, 15, 17, 19, 20, 22, 24, 27, 29 MamasOmar/Shutterstock.com; pp. 4, 5, 6, 8, 12, 14, 16, 18, 20, 28, 30, 31, 32 Dadan Andriyana/Shutterstock.com; p. 5, 10, 22, 26 Kovalov Anatolii/Shutterstock.com; p. 5 Oleksandr Poliashenko/Shutterstock.com; p. 5 Cal Sport Media / Alamy Stock Photo; pp.7, 9, 19 UPI / Alamy Stock Photo; pp. 11, 17 Ringo Chiu/Shutterstock.com; pp. 13, 21, 25 Kirby Lee / Alamy Stock Photo; p. 15 Alonzo J. Adams/Shutterstock.com; pp. 23, 29 Cal Sport Media / Alamy Stock Photo; p. 27 ZUMA Press, Inc. / Alamy Stock Photo.

Printed in the United States of America

CPSIA compliance information: Batch #CSGS26: For further information contact Gareth Stevens, at 1-800-542-2595.

CONTENTS

FUTURE GOAT

Caleb Williams has always set high **goals** for himself. He worked hard to be the best on any team he was on, from high school to the National Football League (NFL). But even when he was a kid, Williams was changing the game on the field.

IN THE POCKET

IN 2023, WILLIAMS TOLD *GQ* THAT HE WANTED TO WIN EIGHT SUPER BOWLS—ONE MORE THAN FOOTBALL GREAT TOM BRADY!

BEARS
18
GSH

ALL IN THE FAMILY

Williams was born on November 18, 2001. His dad, Carl, worked in **real estate** and later became part-owner of a gym. Williams grew up with his dad and his mom, Dayna, near Washington, DC. He doesn't have any brothers or sisters.

CALEB WILLIAMS WITH HIS PARENTS

IN THE POCKET

THE WILLIAMSES ARE A FAMILY OF ATHLETES. CARL WILLIAMS PLAYED COLLEGE FOOTBALL AT OKLAHOMA STATE. DAYNA PLAYED VOLLEYBALL AND BASKETBALL FOR THE UNIVERSITY OF MARYLAND.

STARTING OUT

Williams started playing football at a young age. At first, he played linebacker and running back. He went to football camps to learn more skills. There, he showed he could hit hard! Coaches started playing him against older kids.

IN THE POCKET

EVEN AS A KID, WILLIAMS WOULD MEET FRIENDS AT 5:30 A.M. TO WORK OUT!

At age 10, Williams already didn't like losing. He often cried. Williams wanted to be in control on the field. So, he decided to learn to be a quarterback! It took a lot of time and work. He trained with special coaches for quarterbacks.

IN THE POCKET

WILLIAMS STARTED DOING HOT YOGA TO BE IN GOOD SHAPE FOR FOOTBALL. HOT YOGA IS INTENSE. THE YOGA ROOM IS HEATED TO 80°F (27°C) OR MORE.

HIGH SCHOOL HOTSHOT

By the time Williams started high school, he was a superstar. He beat out older players to become the starting quarterback as a freshman, or first-year student. In 2018, Williams led his team to a **conference** championship.

IN THE POCKET

WILLIAMS HAD ALREADY DONE SOME MEDIA TRAINING BY HIGH SCHOOL. THIS MEANS LEARNING HOW TO TALK TO AND ACT AROUND MEMBERS OF THE MEDIA.

AT OKLAHOMA

Williams finished high school early and started at the University of Oklahoma in 2021. He began playing for Oklahoma Sooners coach Lincoln Riley. Riley had coached many successful quarterbacks. Williams chose Oklahoma partly because of Riley's leadership.

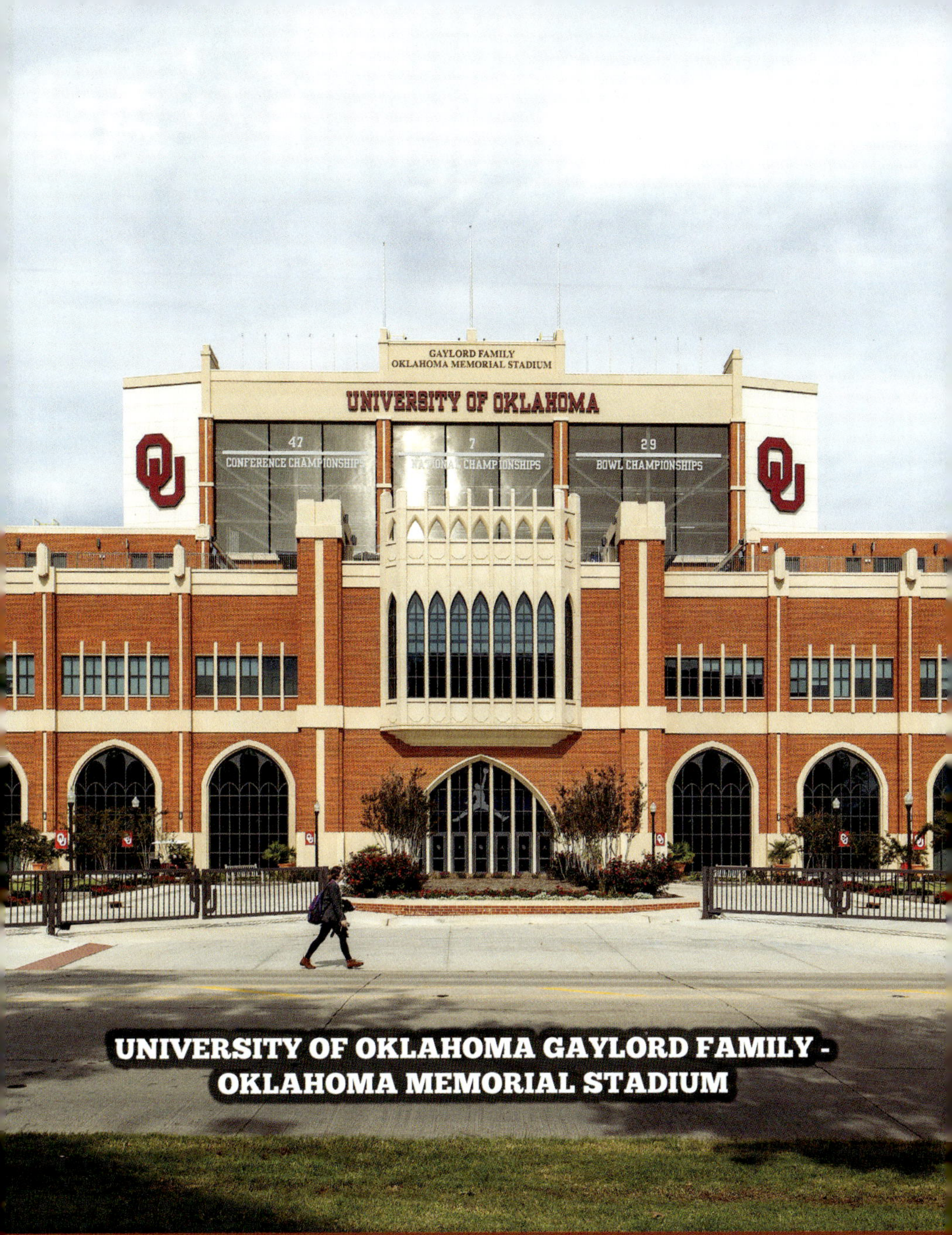

UNIVERSITY OF OKLAHOMA GAYLORD FAMILY - OKLAHOMA MEMORIAL STADIUM

IN THE POCKET

BY THE MIDDLE OF HIS FRESHMAN SEASON, WILLIAMS WAS THE STARTING QUARTERBACK FOR THE SOONERS.

THE SCRAMBLE

Before the end of the season, Riley left Oklahoma to coach at the University of Southern California (USC). Williams decided to join Riley's team at USC when a spot opened up for him. He transferred, or changed schools, to USC in February 2022.

IN THE POCKET

WILLIAMS LATER SAID THAT HE KNEW HE WAS THE RIGHT QUARTERBACK FOR RILEY'S **SYSTEM.** HE WAS HAPPY TO HAVE A SPOT WITH RILEY ON THE USC TEAM.

TROJAN AT THE TOP

In Williams's first year at USC, he led the Trojans to their conference's championship game. Even though they lost, Williams won the Heisman Trophy, or prize, in 2022! The Heisman honors the best college football player in the country.

IN THE POCKET

WILLIAMS SET MANY RECORDS IN THE 2022 SEASON AT USC, INCLUDING A RECORD 4,537 PASSING YARDS AND THE MOST TOUCHDOWNS RUSHING AND PASSING (52).

MONEYMAKER

At USC, Williams became one of the best-paid college athletes of the time. He was one of the early leaders of NIL, or college athletes' ability to make money from use of their name, **image**, and likeness. He had deals with companies like Beats by Dre.

IN THE POCKET

WILLIAMS STARTED PAINTING HIS NAILS BEFORE GAMES WHILE IN HIGH SCHOOL. IT HONORS HIS MOM, WHO HAS LONG WORKED AS A NAIL TECHNICIAN.

Williams continued to show his greatness in the 2023 football season. The Trojans team was less successful that year though. Still, Williams completed a total of 41 touchdowns. His playing got the attention of many teams in the NFL.

IN THE POCKET

SINCE WILLIAMS WON THE HEISMAN, HIS USC NUMBER 13 WAS RETIRED AFTER HE LEFT THE TROJANS. THAT MEANS NO ONE ELSE WILL WEAR THAT NUMBER!

13
PAC 12
SC
DRI-FIT
FIGHT ON!

#NUMBER ONE PICK

Williams entered the NFL **Draft**. If the right team didn't show interest, he would go back to USC for his senior, or last, year. Then, the Chicago Bears came calling. The Bears chose Williams first in the NFL Draft in April 2024!

IN THE POCKET

IN COLLEGE, WILLIAMS KEPT A LIST OF GOALS ON HIS PHONE. BEING THE FIRST PICK IN THE NFL DRAFT WAS ONE OF THEM!

IS ON
NFL
NFLN

TO THE NFL

In September 2024, Williams started as quarterback in his first NFL game—and the Bears won! As the season went on, he kept getting better. He was thought to be one of the best rookies, or first-year players, in the NFL!

IN THE POCKET

BEFORE HIS FIRST GAME, WILLIAMS SAID PREPARING FOR THE SEASON WITH THE BEARS WAS FUN!

GIVING BACK

Williams does more than play football. He's a businessman and is known for wearing cool clothes! He also founded the Caleb Cares Foundation. This group works on anti-bullying projects and other ways to help youth. What will Williams do next?

IN THE POCKET

WILLIAMS LOVES SUPERMAN! HE SAYS THAT THROUGH CALEB CARES HE WANTS KIDS TO BELIEVE THEY ARE SUPERHEROES TOO—AND THAT THEIR DIFFERENCES ARE THEIR SUPERPOWERS.

CALEB WILLIAMS FOOTBALL TIMELINE

2007 Williams starts playing running back and linebacker around age 6.

2011 He decides he wants to play quarterback around age 10.

2017 He becomes the starting quarterback for his high school football team as a freshman.

2018 He leads his high school team to a conference championship.

2021 He starts playing football at the University of Oklahoma.

2022 He starts playing for USC. He wins the Heisman Trophy.

2024 He is the number one pick in the NFL Draft. He plays his first NFL game with the Chicago Bears.

FOR MORE INFORMATION

BOOKS

Roland, James. *The Next Generation: NFL Star Quarterbacks*. San Diego, CA: ReferencePoint Press, 2025.

Stewart, Mark. *The Chicago Bears*. Buffalo, NY: Norwood House Press, 2025.

WEBSITES

Caleb Williams
https://www.chicagobears.com/team/players-roster/caleb-williams/
Keep up with Caleb Williams on the Chicago Bears website.

Caleb Williams
https://calebwilliams13.com
Find out more about Caleb on his website

Publisher's note to educators and parents: Our editors have carefully reviewed these websites to ensure that they are suitable for students. Many websites change frequently, however, and we cannot guarantee that a site's future contents will continue to meet our high standards of quality and educational value. Be advised that students should be closely supervised whenever they access the internet.

GLOSSARY

athlete: A person who is skilled at a sport.

conference: A group of sports teams that compete with each other.

draft: The process of selecting a player from a pool of potential players entering the league.

goal: An end to which someone is working.

image: Face, such as in a photo. Also, how a person is thought of by others or the media.

intense: Existing to an extreme degree.

media: The outlets and people that offer news coverage.

real estate: The buying and selling of homes and properties.

system: A group of similar parts that move or work together.

technician: A person who has special training to do a job.

INDEX